# Homemade Ice Recipes

Helen Amato

# Introduction

I want to thank you and congratulate you for purchasing the book, *"Homemade Ice Cream Recipes."*

Are you tired of buying ice cream and want to make your own at home?

Would you love to always have a nice cold icy treat at your disposal any time you want?

Well, if you are considering making ic cream at home, then this is the right book for you.

When most people think of making ice cream, they think it is one of the hardest tasks; thus, they shy away from it. However, making ice cream at home is relatively easy. It is also a fun activity you can engage in with your kids, and thanks to this book, you will have all the information you need to make tasty delectable homemade ice creams. The amazing thing is that with some recipes, you don't even need an ice cream maker; all you need is a fridge to freeze your ice cream and you are good to go.

Are you ready to get started on learning how to make the best ice creams you have ever tasted?

Well, let us start then.

# Table of Contents

## Introduction _____ 2

## Churned, Homemade Ice Cream Recipes __ 7

*Simple Vanilla Ice Cream _____ 7*

*Cherry Ice Cream _____ 9*

*Kiwi Ice Cream _____ 11*

*Oreo Cookies Ice Cream _____ 13*

*Mint Chocolate Chip Ice Cream _____ 15*

*Green Tea Ice Cream _____ 17*

*Lime Ice Cream _____ 19*

*Cherry Chocolate Chip Ice Cream _____ 21*

*Pecan Ice Cream _____ 24*

*Vanilla Bean Ice Cream _____ 26*

*Vegan Ice Cream _____ 28*

*Orange Ice Cream _____ 30*

# Homemade Ice Cream Recipes

*Peanut Butter Ice Cream* _____ *32*

*Coconut Ice Cream* _____ *34*

*Pumpkin Ice Cream* _____ *36*

*Banana-Caramel Ice Cream* _____ *38*

*Almond Ice Cream* _____ *41*

*Mango Ice Cream* _____ *43*

*Banana Ice Cream* _____ *44*

*Peanut Butter Ice Cream* _____ *46*

*Peachy Ice Cream* _____ *48*

*Fig Ice Cream* _____ *51*

*Purple Ice Cream* _____ *53*

*Prune Ice Cream* _____ *55*

*Blue Moon Ice Cream* _____ *57*

*Rum Ice Cream* _____ *60*

*Strawberry Ice Cream* _____ *62*

## Homemade Ice Cream Recipes

*Cardamom Ice Cream* ............................... 64

*Spicy Ice Cream* ............................... 66

*Corn Ice Cream* ............................... 69

*Feijoa Ice Cream* ............................... 71

**No-Churn Recipes** ............................... **73**

*Mint-Chip Ice Cream* ............................... 73

*Nesquik Frostee Ice Cream* ............................... 75

*Rainbow Ice Cream* ............................... 76

*Pina Colada Ice Cream* ............................... 78

*Tropical Ice Cream* ............................... 80

*Chocolate Peanut Butter Ice Cream* ............................... 82

*Watermelon Ice Cream* ............................... 84

*Oreo Ice Cream* ............................... 85

*Bubblegum Ice Cream* ............................... 86

*Peppermint Ice Cream* ............................... 88

## Homemade Ice Cream Recipes

*Dairy-Free Vanilla Ice Cream* _____ 90

*Blueberry Ice Cream* _____ 92

*Coffee Ice Cream* _____ 94

*Vegan Peanut Butter Ice Cream* _____ 96

*Cookie Butter Ice Cream* _____ 98

*Raspberry Ice Cream* _____ 99

*Snow Ice Cream* _____ 100

*Keto-Coconut Ice Cream* _____ 101

*Unicorn Ice Cream* _____ 103

*Maple Bacon Ice Cream* _____ 105

*Colorful Ice Cream* _____ 107

**Conclusion** _____ **109**

# Churned, Homemade Ice Cream Recipes

## Simple Vanilla Ice Cream

*Prep time: 5 mins*

*Freeze time: 2 hours*

*Total time: 2 hours 5 mins*

### Ingredients

½ cup of sugar

2 cups of thickened cream

1 teaspoon of vanilla

1 cup of full cream milk

### Directions

Place the cream, milk, and sugar in a medium bowl and whisk until the sugar completely dissolves, then mix in the vanilla.

Churn the mixture according to the manufacturer's instructions. Transfer the ice cream to an airtight container and freeze for 2 hours or until the ice cream firms up as desired.

## Cherry Ice Cream

*Prep time: 10 mins*

*Cook time: 10 mins*

*Freeze time: 3 hours*

*Total time: 3 hours 20 mins*

### Ingredients

450 gm of Morello cherries

5 egg yolks

1½ cups of thickened cream

¾ cup of sugar

1 cup of full cream milk

### Directions

In a medium bowl, whisk the yolks and sugar; once pale, set aside.

Pour the milk and cream into a saucepan, place over medium-high heat, bring to a simmer, switch off the heat, and set aside.

Gradually pour and fast-whisk one cup of milk and cream mixture into the sugar and yolk mixture. Once done, pour the sugar, yolks, and milk mixture into the saucepan with milk and cream.

Heat the mixture on medium-high heat —make sure it does not boil— until it thickens, and then remove from heat.

Blitz your cherries and then whip them into the base. Refrigerate the ice cream base for 3 hours or overnight.

Use manufacturer's instructions to churn the ice cream in your ice cream maker.

Transfer into a container and freeze for 3 hours.

Serve topped with berries of choice.

## Kiwi Ice Cream

*Prep time: 10 mins*

*Cook time: 10 mins*

*Freeze time: 3 hours*

*Total time: 3 hours 20 mins*

## Ingredients

5 egg yolks

1 cup of full cream milk

¾ cup of sugar

1 cup of thickened cream

4 peeled and chopped kiwi fruits

## Directions

Place the chopped pieces of kiwi fruit in your blender and blend until smooth.

In a large bowl, whisk together the sugar and egg york; once done, set aside.

Pour the cream and milk into a saucepan over medium-high heat and simmer.

# Homemade Ice Cream Recipes

Gradually pour and whisk one cup of the milk mixture into the egg yolks and sugar mixture and mix gently. Pour the mixture into the milk and cream mixture and heat for 5 minutes or until you acquire the desired thickness.

Strain ice cream base into an airtight container, mix with the blended kiwi fruit, and place in the fridge for 3 hours or overnight for best results.

Transfer the ice cream to an ice cream make and churn following the manufacturer's instructions. Once ready, transfer to a container, and freeze for 2 hours or until the ice cream hardens

Serve garnished with kiwi wedges.

## Oreo Cookies Ice Cream

*Prep time: 5 mins*

*Freeze time: 2 hours*

*Total time: 2 hours 5 mins*

**Ingredients**

1 cup of sugar

1 cup of full cream milk

137g of Oreo cookies

5 drops of blue food color

1 tablespoon of vanilla essence

2 cups of thickened cream

**Directions**

Put the cream, milk, sugar, and vanilla essence in a large bowl and whip until well mixed. Chill the mixture in the fridge for 2 hours.

Churn your ice cream according to your manufacturer's instructions. In the final minute of churning, add in the cookies.

Transfer the mixture into an airtight container and freeze for 2 hours or until hardened to your liking.

## Mint Chocolate Chip Ice Cream

*Prep time: 10 mins*

*Cook time: 10 mins*

*Freeze time: 3 hours*

*Total time: 3 hours 20 mins*

### Ingredients

1½ cups of roughly chopped, fresh mint

1¼ cups of thickened cream

6 egg yolks

100 gm of chocolate chips

½ cup of sugar

1 cup of full cream milk

### Directions

Add the milk, cream, and sugar to a saucepan, and cook over medium-heat until the mixture is simmering, and then set aside.

Put the egg yolks in a large bowl and beat until pale, slowly pour in a cup of the hot milk and keep whipping.

Start pouring the mixture back into the saucepan with the hot milk mixture, gently whisking, and heat for 3-5 minutes until the custard base thickens. Make sure it does not boil. When the milk coats the back of your spoon, it's ready.

Set the custard base aside so that it can cool, then add the custard base and mint to a food processor and process for 6 pulses. Pour the mixture into an airtight container and refrigerate overnight, allowing the mint to infuse properly.

Churn according to the manufacturer's instructions, and add in the chocolate chips towards the end of churning.

Transfer the ice cream into an airtight container and freeze for 2 hours or until the ice cream attains your desired consistency.

## Green Tea Ice Cream

*Prep time: 10 mins*

*Cook time: 20 mins*

*Freeze time: 8 hours*

*Total time: 8 hours 30 mins*

**Ingredients**

¾ cup of whipped heavy cream

¾ cup of whole milk

5 tablespoons of granulated white sugar

2 egg yolks

3 tablespoons of hot water

1 tablespoon of green tea powder

**Directions**

Whisk together the hot water and matcha tea powder in a small bowl and put aside.

Transfer the egg yolks and the sugar to a medium-size saucepan and beat until well mixed. Pour in the milk gradually, whisking to combine well.

Heat the mixture on low heat, constantly stirring to keep it from burning. When the mixture thickens slightly, remove from the heat.

To cool the egg mixture, soak the bottom of the pan in ice water.

Pour in the matcha mixture into the pan, mix well, and continue cooling.

Whip the heavy cream until it's airy and slightly thick. Pour this into the egg-matcha mixture. Use a spatula to whisk the mixture gently until the ingredients combine well.

Churn the ice cream mixture following the manufacturer's instructions. Once done, pour the ice cream mixture into an airtight container and freeze for 8 hours.

# Lime Ice Cream

*Prep time: 10 mins*

*Cook time: 10 mins*

*Freeze time: 3 hours*

*Total time: 3 hours 20 mins*

**Ingredients**

Zest of 5 lemons

1½ cups of full cream milk

¾ cup of sugar

6 egg yolks

4 tablespoons of lime juice

3 drops of green food color

1½ cups of thickened cream

A pinch of kosher salt

**Directions**

Put the egg yolks and sugar into a medium bowl, whisk until pale, and then set aside.

Pour the cream and milk into a large saucepan, heat until simmering, and then turn off the heat and set aside.

Gradually pour a cup of milk into the egg and sugar mixture, and whisk as quickly as you can. Now, pour the yolk mixture into the saucepan with milk and heat on medium heat until the mixture thickens and it can coat the back of the spoon. Once done, remove from heat.

Use a container to stir together the lime juice, salt, and food color, and refrigerate for 2 hours.

Use the manufacturer's instructions to churn, and as the ice cream hardens, add in the lime zest.

Once done churning, transfer the ice cream into an airtight container and freeze for 2 hours.

Scoop, serve, and enjoy.

# Cherry Chocolate Chip Ice Cream

*Prep time: 10 mins*

*Cook time: 20 mins*

*Freeze time: 3 hours*

*Total time: 3 hours 30 mins*

**Ingredients**

*For the Cherry Mixture*

1 tablespoon of water

1½-2 cups of fresh sweet cherries, pitted

3 tablespoons of sugar

*For the Custard*

6 egg yolks from large eggs

1½ cups of whole milk

1½ teaspoon of vanilla extract

1½ cups of heavy cream

2/3 cup of sugar, divided

A dash of salt

***For the chocolate mixture***

2 teaspoons of vegetable oil

3 ounces of semi-sweet chocolate broken into pieces

**Directions**

Place the cherries, 3 tablespoons of sugar, and 1 tablespoon of water into a small saucepan and bring to boil on medium-high heat, making sure to stir constantly until the cherries are soft and syrupy, which should take about 4 to 6 minutes. Once ready, transfer to an airtight container, cover, and refrigerate.

Place the cream, milk, 1/3 cup of sugar, and 1 teaspoon of vanilla extract —you can use bean paste too— into a large saucepan.

Whip the egg yolks, salt, and the remaining 1/3 cup of sugar in a small bowl and place aside.

Place the milk and cream mixture on medium-high heat and cook until it starts to boil. Once boiling, remove from heat. Slowly pour 1 cup of the hot milk into the egg yolk mixture, making sure to whisk consistently.

Pour the egg mixture back in the pan and cook on medium-low heat, stirring until the mixture can coat the back of a spoon —or reaches 160F-180F. Sieve the mixture into a bowl. Cover the bowl and refrigerate for 3 hours.

Churn the custard following the manufacturer's instructions. Halfway through the ice cream-freezing process, simmer some water, place in a bowl, and use this to melt the chocolate and vegetable oil. Once melted, let the mixture cool a bit and then transfer it into a food storage bag. If the mixture hardens before you can use it, use warm water to soften.

Once your ice cream is soft-frozen, slice off a corner of the food storage bag and use this end to squeeze the chocolate out of the bag and into the ice cream maker. As the ice cream churns and hardens, the chocolate will harden too and create chocolate chips.

Once done churning, transfer into a freezer-safe container and freeze covered for 30 minutes. While the ice cream is still soft, tuck or swirl in the cherries and refrigerate until you get the desired consistency.

## Pecan Ice Cream

*Prep time: 30 mins*

*Cook time: 5 mins*

*Freeze time: 10 hours*

*Total time: 10 hours 35 mins*

### Ingredients

2 cups of heavy whipping cream

¾ cup of honey

1 cup of chopped pecans

1½ tablespoons of vanilla extract

2 cups of milk

2 tablespoons of butter

### Directions

Pour the honey into a large saucepan and warm.

Add in the milk, whipping cream, vanilla extract, and mix until well combined.

Pour the mixture into an airtight container and refrigerate for 8 hours before proceeding to churn. Before you start churning, place the butter in a large skillet and melt over medium-high heat. Add in the pecans, sauté until lightly brown, and then let this cool completely.

Churn the chilled ice cream following the manufacturer's instructions. Add the cooled butter pecans to the machine 15 minutes into churning.

Once done churning, freeze the churned ice cream in a freezer-safe container for 2 hours.

Serve and enjoy.

## Vanilla Bean Ice Cream

*Prep time: 10 mins*

*Cook time: 10 mins*

*Freeze time: 3 hours*

*Total time: 3 hours 20 mins*

**Ingredients**

6 egg yolks

¾ cup of sugar

1 vanilla bean

1 pinch of kosher salt

1 teaspoon of vanilla essence

½ cup of thickened cream

1½ cups of full cream milk

**Directions**

Add milk, cream, sugar to a saucepan, and cook on medium-high heat. Bring to a simmer, then remove from heat.

Whisk the egg yolks until pale, then gradually pour in a cup of the hot mixture and whisk continuously.

Transfer the egg and milk mixture into the saucepan with the hot milk, and keep whisking until mixed. Add the salt, vanilla essence, scraped vanilla bean, and vanilla pod into the mixture and heat for 3 minutes on medium-high heat, allowing the liquid to thicken. Transfer the mixture to an airtight container and refrigerate for 3 hours or overnight.

Strain the custard through a fine sieve into the bowl of an ice cream maker. Churn the ice cream using the manufacturer's instructions. Transfer the churned ice cream to an airtight container and freeze for 3 hours.

## Vegan Ice Cream

*Prep time: 14 mins*

*Total time: 1 hour 40 mins*

### Ingredients

¾ cup of sugar

13.5 ounces of coconut milk

3 tablespoons of fresh lemon juice

¼ teaspoon of xanthan gum (optional)

¼ teaspoon of kosher salt

½ teaspoon of lemon zest

2 medium-sized avocados, halved, pitted, and peeled

### Directions

Place the avocados in a bowl and mash; you should have 1½ cups of mashed avocados.

Add the avocados, lemon zest and juice, coconut milk, xanthan gum (optional), sugar, salt, and ¼ cup of water to a blender and blend into a smooth consistency.

Put the mixture in a freezer-safe container and refrigerate for 1 hour. Use the manufacturer's instructions to churn and freeze the ice cream mixture.

Transfer the ice cream to a loaf pan, wrap in plastic wrap, and freeze until hardened —up to a week.

Before serving, let the ice cream sit at room temperature for 20 minutes and then scoop into serving dishes.

## Orange Ice Cream

*Prep time: 20 mins*

*Total time: 50 mins*

### Ingredients

Zest of 6 oranges

2 cups of heavy cream

2 cups of skim milk

1 cup of sugar

8 large egg yolks

¼ teaspoon of coarse salt

### Directions

Whip together the egg yolks, sugar, and salt in a saucepan until well mixed, then gradually whip in the milk.

Place the saucepan over medium-high heat and cook, constantly stirring until the custard can coat the back of a wooden spoon, which should take 10 to 12 minutes.

Whisk the orange zest into the custard and let this sit covered for 30 minutes.

Strain the custard through a fine sieve into a bowl and place the bowl over ice water.

Pour in the cream and stir several times until chilled.

Follow the manufacturer's instructions to churn the ice cream, then transfer to an airtight container and freeze for 2 hours.

## Peanut Butter Ice Cream

*Prep time: 10 mins*

*Freeze time: 5 hours*

*Total time: 5 hours 10 mins*

### Ingredients

1 cup of chopped peanut butter cups

1/3 cup of creamy peanut butter

1 1/3 cups of heavy whipping cream

1/8 teaspoon of kosher salt

1 teaspoon of vanilla extract

1/3 cup of granulated sugar

### Directions

Add the cream, sugar, peanut butter, vanilla, and salt to a blender and blend until smooth.

Refrigerate the mixture for 1 hour.

Use the manufacturer's instructions to churn the chilled mixture, and towards the end of the churning process, add in the peanut butter cups.

# Homemade Ice Cream Recipes

Put in the freezer for 4 hours or until firm.

## Coconut Ice Cream

*Prep time: 15 mins*

*Freeze time: 3 hours*

*Total time: 3 hours 15 mins*

**Ingredients**

6 large egg yolks

¼ teaspoon of kosher salt

1 cup of sugar

2 cups of heavy cream

¼ cup of sweetened coconut, shredded

2 cups of skim milk

1 cup of unsweetened, toasted coconut flakes

**Directions**

Add the milk, cream, unsweetened coconut, and salt to a saucepan and stir well. Place over heat and bring to a simmer. Once simmering, set aside and let it cool for 2 hours as you prepare an ice water bath.

Return the milk mixture to heat, whisk in a ½ cup of sugar, and simmer.

Beat the egg yolks and the remaining ½ cup of sugar in a bowl and gradually whip in half the milk mixture into the egg yolk mixture.

Pour the mixture back in the pan and cook over medium-high heat, constantly stirring for 6 minutes until the custard can coat back of a wooden spoon.

Strain the custard through a fine sieve into a bowl and place it on the ice water bath. Allow the custard to chill, stirring occasionally.

Following the manufacturer's instructions, freeze the custard in the ice cream maker and churn until the ice cream is soft and able to hold its shape when you turn the machine off.

Transfer to a loaf pan and sprinkle with sweetened coconut. You can eat the ice cream as is, soft, or freeze until the ice cream attains your desired consistency.

If you decide to freeze, let the ice cream rest at room temperature for 10 minutes before serving.

## Pumpkin Ice Cream

*Prep time: 10 mins*

*Cook time: 10 mins*

*Freeze time: 3 hours*

*Total time: 3 hours 20 mins*

### Ingredients

1 cup of pumpkin puree

6 egg yolks

½ teaspoon of ground cinnamon

1 cup of thickened cream

½ teaspoon of vanilla extract

1/3 cup of caster sugar

2 tablespoons of dark brown sugar

1½ cups of full-cream milk

### Directions

In a medium bowl, beat the egg yolks and sugar until pale, then put aside.

# Homemade Ice Cream Recipes

Pour the cream and milk into a saucepan and cook on medium-high heat, stirring consistently, bring to a simmer, and then set aside.

Gradually add a cup of the hot milk mixture to the yolk and sugar mix and whip as fast as you can. Pour the egg yolk and milk mixture back into the pan with hot milk mixture.

Place the saucepan on your stove and cook on medium heat until the mixture thickens, and it can coat the back of a spoon, then remove from heat.

Pour the milk mixture, pumpkin, brown sugar, vanilla, and cinnamon into a blender and process for 1 minute.

Transfer the ice cream custard into an airtight container and refrigerate for 2-3 hours or until cooled.

Follow your manufacturer's instructions to churn the ice cream, and then pour it into a freezer-safe container. Freeze for no less than 3 hours or until the ice cream hardens to your desired consistency.

## Banana-Caramel Ice Cream

*Prep time: 20 mins*

*Freeze time: 5 hours*

*Total time: 5 hours 20 mins*

### Ingredients

1½ cups of overripe, mashed bananas

½ stick of unsalted butter, cut into small chunks

1 2/3 cups of sugar, divided

4 large egg yolks

1 tablespoon of light corn syrup

1 teaspoon of salt, divided

¼ cup of water

1 teaspoon of pure vanilla extract

1 2/3 cups of heavy cream, plus ½ cup, divided

1 2/3 cups of whole milk

## Directions

Vigorously beat the egg yolks and 2/3 cup of sugar for 2 minutes until slightly fluffy and set aside

Pour the milk and 2/3 cup of cream in a medium-sized saucepan and bring to a boil, then remove from heat.

Slowly whip the milk mixture into the egg mixture and transfer the now-acquired mixture back into the saucepan.

Cook the mixture for 1 minute on medium-high heat, occasionally stirring with a heat-safe spatula, until it thickens and it can coat the back of the spatula. Make sure the mixture does not boil.

Transfer the custard into a bowl, and set it in an ice-water bath, making sure to stir as it cools. Pour half of the cooled custard and the bananas in a blender and process until smooth; pour this in the bowl with remaining custard.

Mix in vanilla, ¼ teaspoon of salt, 1 cup of the cream, and stir well.

Strain the custard through a fine sieve into a medium-sized bowl, and refrigerate for 2 hours or overnight for best results.

Add water, corn syrup, and the remaining sugar to a saucepan. Place the saucepan on medium-high heat, and bring to a simmer, swirling the pan occasionally without stirring.

Continue cooking on high heat for 9 minutes, making sure to swirl the pan until the mixture has a deep amber color. Remove from heat, gradually add the remaining cream, remaining salt, and simmer the caramel for 1 minute. Place the pan in an ice-water bath to cool; make sure it doesn't become too cold such that it can't melt the butter. After cooling for a while, whip in the butter chunks one at a time, whisking until well mixed.

Freeze a 5*10-inch loaf pan for 10 minutes.

Follow the manufacturer's instructions to churn and freeze the ice cream. Use a third of the ice cream custard to make a layer in the loaf pan, and then layer on one-third of the caramel. Use a wooden skewer to swirl the caramel into the ice cream. Continue layering until you have no more ice cream or caramel to layer.

Freeze for 4 hours or until firm to your desired consistency.

## Almond Ice Cream

*Prep time: 10 mins*

*Cook time: 10 mins*

*Freeze time: 2 hours*

*Total time: 2 hours 20 mins*

### Ingredients

300ml of full-fat milk

125g of almonds

300ml of cream

100g of sugar

3 egg yolks

### Directions

Whip the egg yolks until they turn pale, then put aside.

Grill almonds on an oven tray for 5 mins until brown, then set aside to cool.

Add milk, cream, and sugar to a saucepan and bring to a simmer, then remove from heat.

Slowly pour and whisk a cup of the milk mixture into the yolks. Transfer the yolk and egg mixture to the saucepan and heat until a thick custard forms.

Strain the custard through a fine strainer into a bowl and add the almonds. Process in a blender until you have a smooth consistency.

Pour the smooth custard into an airtight container and refrigerate for 2 hours.

Follow the manufacturer's instructions to churn the ice cream, then put in a container and freeze to desired hardness.

# Mango Ice Cream

*Prep time: 10 mins*

*Cook time: 10 mins*

*Freeze time: 3 hours*

*Total time: 3 hours 20 mins*

## Ingredients

2 cups of thickened cream

1 cup of full cream milk

¾ cup of sugar

1 cup of fresh or frozen mango

## Directions

Put the mango in a blender, blend, and then refrigerate for an hour. Whip the sugar, cream, and milk until well mixed. Churn the mixture following the manufacturer's instructions.

Towards the end of the churning process, add in the mango. Transfer the ice cream to an airtight container and freeze for 2 hours —more if necessary.

## Banana Ice Cream

*Prep time: 10 mins*

*Cook time: 10 mins*

*Freeze time: 3 hours*

*Total time: 3 hours 20 mins*

### Ingredients

1¼ cups of thickened cream

2 tablespoons of softened butter

3 ripe bananas, roughly chopped

4 egg yolks

A pinch of kosher salt

½ cup of sugar

1 cup of full cream milk

¾ cup of brown sugar

### Directions

Place your banana, brown sugar, and butter in a skillet, and cook on low-medium heat; once the bananas cook through, remove from heat.

Add milk, cream, sugar to a saucepan; turn your stove to medium-high heat, place the saucepan over the heat, bring to a simmer, and then remove from heat.

Beat the egg yolks until pale in color, then gradually pour one cup of the milk into the yolks. Transfer the yolk and milk mixture back in the saucepan and whip until you have a custard base.

Heat the custard base on medium-high heat, making sure it does not boil; this should take about 5 minutes. Once the custard can coat the back of a mixing spoon, it's ready.

Use your blender to blitz the custard and the bananas until well mixed. Transfer the mixture into an airtight container and refrigerate for 3 hours or overnight.

Follow the manufacturer's instructions to churn the ice cream. Once done, transfer to an airtight container and freeze for 2 hours or until the ice cream attains the desired consistency.

Serve garnished with bananas slices.

## Peanut Butter Ice Cream

*Prep time: 10 mins*

*Cook time: 10 mins*

*Freeze time: 3 hours*

*Total time: 3 hours 20 mins*

### Ingredients

6 large egg yolks

½ cup of sugar

½ cup of peanut butter

1 cup of full-cream milk

1 teaspoon of vanilla

1 cup of thickened cream

### Directions

Pour milk and cream into a saucepan and cook over medium-high heat, stirring the mixture consistently. Bring to a simmer and remove from heat.

Whisk the egg yolks and sugar, making sure they combine well.

Gradually pour a cup of the hot milk mixture into the egg mix, making sure to whisk continuously.

Pour the yolk mixture into the saucepan with hot milk. Add the peanut butter and cook until the mixture thickens, making sure it does not boil.

Transfer the custard into an airtight container and refrigerate for 3 hours or overnight for the best results.

Use the manufacturer's instructions to churn the ice cream custard, then transfer it into an airtight container, and proceed to freeze for 2 hours or until the ice cream hardens.

## Peachy Ice Cream

*Prep time: 30 mins*

*Total time: 3 hours 15 mins*

### Ingredients

2-3 peeled, pitted, and sliced peaches

8 large egg yolks

2 teaspoons of vanilla extract

1 tablespoon of fresh lemon juice

¾ cup of sugar

1 cup of whole milk

½ teaspoon of kosher salt

1 cup of heavy cream

### Directions

Pour the cream and milk into a medium-sized saucepan and heat over medium-high heat for 2 to 3 minutes or until tiny bubbles start forming around the edges of the saucepan.

As that happens, rapidly whisk together the egg yolks, sugar, and salt for 2 minutes or until thick.

Gradually pour the hot milk mixture into the egg-yolks mixture, and whisk constantly.

Pour the mixture back in the saucepan and heat over medium-high heat, constantly mixing, until the mixture can coat the back of the spoon, which should take 5 to 7 mins. The foam should subside, and the mixture should thicken.

Strain the mixture through a fine-mesh sieve into another bowl, then place the bowl in an ice-water bath. As the mixture cools, prepare the peaches.

Place the peaches and 2 tablespoons of water in a skillet and heat over medium-high heat, bringing to boil. Lower the heat to medium, and simmer, occasionally stirring, until the peaches cook and turn soft, which should take approximately 10-12 minutes. Allow the peaches to cool for 5 minutes.

Transfer the peaches and any additional juice to a blender and puree until smooth; this should make at least 1½ cups of puree. Add the peach puree, lemon juice, and vanilla into the ice cream custard and mix well. Wrap with plastic wrap and refrigerate for 2 hours.

Churn the ice cream following the manufacturer's instructions. Once done, serve.

If you prefer a harder consistency, transfer the ice cream to a loaf pan, wrap firmly with plastic cling, and then freeze for no more than a week. Before serving, let the ice cream sit at room temperature for 15-20 mins.

## Fig Ice Cream

*Prep time: 20 mins*

*Cook time: 30 mins*

*Freeze time: 2 hours*

*Total time: 2 hours 50 mins*

## Ingredients

1½ cups of milk

4 egg yolks

1½ cups of cream

½ cup of sugar

2 tablespoons of honey

500g of fresh, ripe figs

## Directions

Cut the figs in quarters and de-stem them. Place the de-stemmed figs in an over tray and then drizzle on the honey. Roast the figs at 180 degres C for 30 minutes.

Transfer the figs to a blender and process into the desired texture; if you'd like chunks in your ice cream, pulse for a few seconds. If you prefer a smoother consistency, blend for longer. Once done blending, let itcool for a while, transfer into a container, and place in the fridge for later use.

Place the egg yolks and sugar in a medium-sized bowl, then beat and set aside.

Pour the milk and cream into a saucepan placed over medium-high heat, simmer, and then remove from heat.

Slowly pour one cup of the hot milk into the egg yolks mixture, all the while constantly whisking. Pour the mixture back into the pan and simmer on medium heat until the mixture can coat the back of a spoon.

Transfer the mixture into an airtight container and chill in the fridge for 2 hours.

Add the figs to the mixture and churn according to the manufacturer's instructions.

## Purple Ice Cream

*Prep time: 10 mins*

*Cook time: 10 mins*

*Freeze time: 2 hours*

*Total time: 2 hours 20 mins*

### Ingredients

1 ¼ cups of granulated sugar

1 cup of water

3 cups of heavy cream

1½ tablespoons of purple yam extract

2 tablespoons of powdered purple yam

1½ cups of whole milk

### Directions

Freeze the bowl of your ice cream maker overnight.

Mix the powdered purple yam with water in a saucepan.

Simmer the mixture, stirring until it thickens. Switch off the heat, place aside, and allow the mixture to cool completely.

As the mixture cools, whip the milk and granulated sugar in a bowl until the sugar dissolves. Pour in the heavy cream and purple yam extra and stir.

**NOTE:** *The color of the mixture varies depending on the brand of powder used. To improve the hue, you can add purple or violet food color.*

Pour the cooled mixture into the milk and sugar mixture and mix until well combined.

Use the manufacturer's instructions for your ice cream maker to churn for 25 minutes, making sure the ice cream is soft and creamy.

For a firmer consistency, scoop the ice cream into an airtight container and freeze for 2 hours.

Once ready, scoop, and enjoy.

# Prune Ice Cream

*Prep time: 5 mins*

*Cook time: 10 mins*

*Freeze time: 3 hours*

*Total time: 3 hours 15 mins*

## Ingredients

6 egg yolks

1 cup of prunes

2 cups of thickened cream

½ cup of water

1 cup of sugar and ½ cup extra

A pinch of kosher salt

1 cup of full cream milk

## Directions

Pour the water, prunes, and 1 cup of sugar into a saucepan and bring to a boil. Once boiling, reduce the heat to low and simmer for 10 minutes until prunes expand and are soft. Strain the mixture and set aside so that the prunes can cool.

In another bowl, whip together the egg yolks and the extra ½ cup of sugar and then place aside.

Pour the cream and the milk into a saucepan and bring to a simmer. Once simmering, turn off the heat and set aside.

Gradually pour and whisk 1 cup of the milk and cream mixture into the sugar and yolk mixture, making sure the two combine well. Once mixed, slowly pour the mixture into the saucepan with the milk and cream mixture and whisk well while heating until the mixture thickens. Add the salt, whisk well, and transfer from the heat.

Place the prunes and the milk mixture in a blender and process into your desired consistency —if you prefer having some bits of prunes in your ice cream, pulse or blend for no more than a few seconds.

Refrigerate the ice cream custard for 3 hours or overnight. Use your ice cream maker to churn your ice cream.

Once done churning, transfer into a container and keep in the freezer for 2 hours.

## Blue Moon Ice Cream

*Prep time: 10 mins*

*Cook time: 10 mins*

*Freeze time: 3 hours*

*Total time: 3 hours 20 mins*

### Ingredients

1 cup of whole milk

2 cups of heavy cream

2 egg yolks

Blue food coloring

½ cup of sugar

½ teaspoon of vanilla extract

1 tablespoon of instant vanilla pudding mix

1 teaspoon of lemon extract

1 teaspoon of raspberry flavoring

## Directions

Before making the ice cream, place the bowl of your ice cream maker in the freeze overnight.

Lightly whisk the egg yolks and ¼ cup of sugar in a medium-sized bowl and set aside.

Put the cream, milk, and the remaining ¼ cup of sugar in a medium saucepan, whisk and cook on medium-low heat until bubbles form on the pan's edges, then put aside.

Add the warm cream mixture, a tablespoon at a time, to the egg mixture, constantly whipping so that the eggs can temper.

Pour the new mixture back into the saucepan and heat over medium-low heat, making sure to stir occasionally until a coat forms at the back of the spoon

**NOTE:** The above should be between 170-175 degrees F; make sure the mixture does not overheat.

Pour the ice cream custard into a medium bowl and whip in the vanilla pudding until well mixed. Add in the lemon extract, raspberry flavoring, vanilla extract, and the blue food color and whip well until you achieve the desired color.

Leave the mixture to cool for an hour, making sure you frequently stir before freezing.

Cover the bowl and refrigerate the mixture overnight.

Churn the custard for 30 minutes following the manufacturer instructions, and then transfer the ice cream into a container that holds up to a quart, cover and freeze for 3 hours. Once ready, scoop, serve, and enjoy.

## Rum Ice Cream

*Prep time:30 mins*

*Cook time:15 mins*

*Freeze time: 10 hours*

*Total time: 10 hours 45 mins*

**Ingredients**

2 cups of dark raisins

1 tablespoon of vanilla extract

12 egg yolks

2 cups of milk

1 ¼ cups of dark rum, divided

2 cups of heavy whipping cream

2/3 cup of sugar

**Directions**

Whisk together the egg yolks and the sugar in a large saucepan, and then gradually whip in the heavy cream and the milk.

# Homemade Ice Cream Recipes

Place the saucepan on low heat and continue whipping until the mixture slightly thickens, making sure it does not come to a boil and then set aside to cool.

Add in the vanilla extract and a ¼ cup of the rum, then let the mixture cool off completely.

Transfer the custard base into an airtight container and refrigerate for 8 hours.

Place the remaining cup of rum and raisins in a small saucepan and cook on low heat for 5 minutes. Once done, set aside and let it cool completely, allowing the raisings to plump and absorb the rum.

Use your manufacturer's instructions to churn the frozen custard base.

15-minutes into the churning process, add in the plumped rum raisins in the machine and continue churning.

Once ready, scoop the churned ice cream into a freezer-friendly container and freeze for 2 hours.

Serve and enjoy.

## Strawberry Ice Cream

*Prep time: 20 mins*

*Total time: 8 hours 30 mins*

### Ingredients

1 cup of low-fat milk

¼ cup of vodka or silver tequila

½ teaspoon of kosher salt

1 cup of heavy cream

½ cup of light corn syrup

3 cups of hulled and halved strawberries, and an extra 8-ounces of coarsely chopped strawberries

2/3 cup of sugar, and an additional ½ a cup for macerating

1 tablespoon of freshly-squeezed lemon juice

### Directions

Blend the halved strawberries with the lemon juice and salt, then strain through a fine sieve. You'll need 1½ cups of this puree; if you get more than than this, reserve for other uses.

# Homemade Ice Cream Recipes

In a medium saucepan mix the milk, cream, the 2/3 cup of sugar and the corn syrup; once done mixing, bring to a boil.

Lower the heat, simmer for 2 minutes and then pour the mixture into a bowl.

Place the bowl in an ice bath, let it sit for 5 minutes, making sure you occasionally stir until the mixture is cold.

Pour in the strawberry puree, mix well, then cover and refrigerate for 2 hours.

Combine the remaining ½ cup of sugar and Vodka. Add in the chopped strawberries and macerate for 2 hours at room temperature

**NOTE**: You can also cover and macerate in the refrigerator for up to 12 hours.

Use the manufacturer's instructions to process (churn) the puree mixture. Once you get a soft texture, drain the macerated berries, and reserve the syrup.

Fold the macerated berries into the ice cream, then transfer into a loaf pan, cover with plastic wrap, and freeze for 4 hours.

Before serving, let the mixture rest at room temperature for 10 minutes and then serve.

## Cardamom Ice Cream

*Prep time: 20 mins*

*Total time: 3 hours*

### Ingredients

6 egg yolks (from large eggs)

¾ cup of sugar

¼ teaspoon of kosher salt

3 cups of heavy cream

1/3 cup of green cardamom pods

1½ cups of whole milk

***For Serving***

Almond Cookies

Roasted peaches

### Directions

Mix the cream, milk, cardamom pods, in a saucepan and cook over medium-high heat for 2 minutes, occasionally stirring, then remove from heat.

Beat the egg yolks with sugar and salt in a large heatproof bowl until smooth.

Scoop half of the cream mixture into the yolk mixture, a little at a time, constantly whisking until well mixed.

Pour the mixture into the saucepan with the remaining cream mixture and combine well.

Making sure to stir consistently, cook the mixture over medium heat until it can coat the back of the wooden spoon, which should take 5 to 7 minutes.

Strain the custard through a medium-mesh sieve into a bowl and place the bowl over an ice-water bath, making sure to stir frequently for 10 minutes as the custard cools.

Using the manufacturer's instructions, churn the custard into a soft texture. Transfer the ice cream to an airtight container and freeze for 4 hours.

If the ice cream hardens too much, refrigerate for 20 minutes before serving and serve garnished with the peaches and cookies.

## Spicy Ice Cream

*Prep time: 30 mins*

*Cook time: 10 mins*

*Freeze time: 3 hours*

*Total time: 3 hours 40 mins*

### Ingredients

4 egg yolks

1 tablespoon Sichuan pepper

2 cinnamon sticks

1 teaspoon of nutmeg

1 teaspoon of ground cloves

2 star anise

1 teaspoon of vanilla

1 teaspoon of salt

1½ cups of full cream milk

1½ cups of thickened cream

1 cup of sugar

1 tablespoon of skim milk powder

**Directions**

In a medium saucepan, add milk, cream, milk powder, sugar, salt, spices, and cook on medium-high heat, stirring occasionally. Bring to a simmer, then remove from heat.

Allow the mixture to cool before transferring into an airtight container and refrigerate overnight, to allow the flavors to infuse.

The following day, strain the mixture into a saucepan; place the saucepan on medium-high heat and bring to a simmer.

Whip the egg yolks until they turn light in color, then gradually pour a cup of the milk mixture into the egg yolks, all the while stirring. Transfer the egg mixture back into the milk mixture and keep mixing constantly.

Cook the mixture until the liquid can coat back of your stirring spoon, making sure it does not boil, then remove from heat.

Whip in the vanilla and allow to cool. Once cooled, transfer the mixture into an airtight container and refrigerate for 3 hours.

Use the manufacturer's instructions to churn the ice cream, then transfer it into a container. Freeze for 3 hours or until the ice cream attains your desired hardness.

## Corn Ice Cream

*Prep time: 5 mins*

*Cook time: 10 mins*

*Freeze time: 3 hours*

*Total time: 3 hours 15 mins*

**Ingredients**

1¼ cups of thickened cream

3 corn cobs

4 egg yolks

¾ cup of full cream milk

1 teaspoon of vanilla extract

¾ cup of sugar

**Directions**

Whip the egg yolks with sugar until you get a pale mixture, then put aside.

Put the cream and milk in a large saucepan and simmer on medium-high heat, then remove from heat.

Gradually pour ½ cup of the hot milk mixture into the egg and sugar mix, making sure to whisk continuously.

Gradually pour the egg and milk mixture in the saucepan with the milk and cream and cook on medium heat. Add the off-the-cob corn kernels into the saucepan and heat until thick enough to coat the back of your spoon, making sure it does not boil.

Remove from heat and allow the mixture to cool before pouring into an airtight container and refrigerating overnight.

The following day, strain the mixture and pour it into an ice cream maker and use manufacturer's instructions to churn the custard. Put in an airtight container, then freeze for about 3 hours or until hard.

## Feijoa Ice Cream

*Prep time: 10 mins*

*Cook time: 10 mins*

*Freeze time: 3 hours*

*Total time: 3 hours 20 mins*

### Ingredients

1 cup of caster sugar

2 tablespoons of no less than 40% Vodka

1 cup of full cream milk

1 teaspoon of vanilla

1 cup of peeled Feijoas

2 cups of thickened cream

### Directions

Place all the ingredients in a blender and process until well combined.

Follow the manufacturer's instructions to churn the blended mixture.

Transfer the churned mixture into an airtight container and freeze for 3 hours.

# No-Churn Recipes

## Mint-Chip Ice Cream

*Prep time: 15 mins*

*Total time: 6 hours 15 mins*

### Ingredients

1 cup of bittersweet chocolate with at least 70% cacao, chopped

2 cups of chilled heavy cream

1 tablespoon of crème de menthe

2 teaspoons of peppermint extract

1 pinch of kosher salt

14-ounces of sweetened condensed milk

### Directions

Stir together the condensed milk, peppermint extract, and crème de menthe in a large bowl.

Use another bowl to whisk together the heavy cream and salt until firm peaks form.

Working in two batches, gently fold the cream into the milk mixture until can no streaks are visible, then fold in the chocolate.

Pour the mixture into a loaf pan and freeze for 6 hours. The ice cream can keep for a month.

## Nesquik Frostee Ice Cream

*Prep time: 5 mins*

*Total time: 4 hours 10 mins*

### Ingredients

1/3 cup of Nesquik Chocolate Flavor Powder

14.5 oz. can of sweetened condensed milk

3 cups of heavy cream

### Directions

Whisk the heavy cream for 5-6 minutes until firm peaks form, add in the milk, and the Nesquik.

Freeze the mixture in a loaf pan for 4 hours.

Serve dusted with Nesquik powder.

## Rainbow Ice Cream

*Prep time: 10 mins*

*Freeze time: 3 hours*

*Total time: 3 hours 10 mins*

### Ingredients

2 cups of thickened cream

Blue, yellow, green, and pink food color

¼ cup of sprinkles and candy to decorate

1 teaspoon of vanilla

500ml cream

1 (397g) can of condensed milk

### Directions

Mix the condensed milk and vanilla.

In another bowl, whisk the cream until stiff peaks form then fold the milk and vanilla into the cream.

Scoop the mixture into bowls and then to each, add a few drops of the different food coloring.

## Homemade Ice Cream Recipes

Empty the individual bowls, one at a time, into a bigger container, making desired patterns.

Sprinkle on candies like M&Ms and sprinkles of choice; use cling wrap to cover and freeze for 3 hours.

## Pina Colada Ice Cream

*Prep time: 10 mins*

*Cook time: 5 mins*

*Freeze time: 3 hours*

*Total time: 3 hours 15 mins*

**Ingredients**

80ml of Malibu white rum

100g of icing sugar

500ml of thickened cream

125ml of pineapple juice

2 teaspoons of lime juice

75g of shredded coconut for garnishing

**Directions**

In a bowl, pour in the pineapple juice, Malibu rum, and lime juice.

Add the icing sugar and whip until well mixed. Beat in the cream until soft peaks form.

Transfer the ice cream to an airtight container and freeze for 2 hours.

Serve sprinkled with coconut.

## Tropical Ice Cream

*Prep time: 10 mins*

*Freeze time: 3 hours*

*Total time: 3 hours 10 mins*

### Ingredients

2 cans of coconut cream

Zest of 2 limes

Juice of 4 limes

2 tablespoons of coconut oil

2 teaspoons of vanilla extract

4 avocados, peeled and pitted

½ teaspoon of kosher salt

1 cup of maple syrup

½ lime, thinly sliced into quarters, to garnish

### Directions

Place all the ingredients, except lime slices, in a blender and process until smooth.

Transfer the mixture to a loaf pan;, garnish with the lime slices, and freeze for 3 hours.

## Chocolate Peanut Butter Ice Cream

*Prep time: 5 mins*

*Freeze time: 3 hours*

*Total time: 3 hours 5 mins*

**Ingredients**

½ cup of peanut butter

13.5oz can of full-fat coconut milk

½ cup of powdered allulose —you can also use any other powdered sweetener

¼ cup of cocoa powder

1 pinch of kosher salt

1/3 cup of liquid coconut oil

**Directions**

Place all the ingredients in a blender and blend until smooth.

Transfer the mixture into a 2-liter freezer-friendly container, cover and freeze for 30 minutes, then stir the mixture, starting from the sides to the center.

Cover again, and put back in the freezer for another 30minutes, then mix again.

Place back in the freezer for 2-3 hours.

# Watermelon Ice Cream

*Prep time: 10 mins*

*Freeze time: 4 hours*

*Total time: 4 hours 10 mins*

**Ingredients**

2 tablespoons of sugar

¼ teaspoon of vanilla extract

2 cups of whole milk

2 cups of cubed watermelon

**Directions**

Add all the ingredients to a blender and process until smooth. Transfer to a loaf pan and freeze for 3 hours.

Pour the mixture back into the blender and blend once more. Put back in the loaf pan and freeze for 1 hour.

Serve garnished with watermelon wedges.

# Oreo Ice Cream

*Prep time: 15 mins*

*Freeze time: 5 hours*

*Total time: 5 hours 15 mins*

## Ingredients

14-oz. can of condensed milk

30 crushed Oreos, plus more for topping

¼ cup of chocolate sauce, plus more for topping

¼ cup of caramel, plus more for topping

3 cups of heavy cream

## Directions

Whip the cream well until stiff peaks form. Add in the condensed milk and Oreos and fold in until well mixed. Drizzle the caramel and chocolate sauce into the mixture and stir until well mixed.

Put the mixture in a 9x5-inch loaf pan, top with more Oreos, drizzle with caramel and more sauce, and freeze for 5 hours.

Allow ice cream to soften for 10 minutes before serving.

## Bubblegum Ice Cream

*Prep time: 5 mins*

*Freeze time: 3 hours*

*Total time: 3 hours 5 mins*

### Ingredients

40 gumballs

5 drops of pink food color

14-oz. can of condensed milk

5 drops of bubblegum flavor

2 cups of thickened cream

### Directions

Place all the ingredients in a bowl except for the gumballs and whisk until stiff peaks form.

Transfer half of the mixture to a shallow container and smoothen it.

Put half of the gumballs onto the smoothened ice cream, layer the rest of the ice cream, and top with the remaining gumballs.

Wrap the container well with cling and freeze for 3 hours or until hardened.

## Peppermint Ice Cream

*Prep time: 15 mins*

*Freeze time: 6 hours*

*Total time: 6 hours 15 mins*

### Ingredients

14-oz. of sweetened condensed milk

2/3 cup of peppermint bark, crumbled

½ cup of miniature semi-sweet chocolate chips

1 teaspoon vanilla extract

4 miniature candy canes, crushed

3 cups of heavy cream

### Directions

Whisk the cream for 3 minutes until still peaks form, then mix in the condensed milk and vanilla until well combined.

Add in the crushed candy canes, stirring until well mixed, and the candy canes start leaving pink streaks in the custard.

In a different bowl, mix the peppermint bark and chocolate, then fold some of it into the ice cream, making sure to set aside some for garnishing.

Transfer the ice cream into a loaf pan, and top with the remaining chips and bark.

Freeze for 6 hours or until firm.

## Dairy-Free Vanilla Ice Cream

*Prep time: 30 mins*

*Freeze time: 2 hours 30 mins*

*Total time: 3 hours*

**Ingredients**

2/3 cup of water

1 teaspoon of apple cider vinegar

1½ cups of sugar

3½ cups of soymilk

1 tablespoon of vanilla

1½ cups of soymilk powder

**Directions**

Add the soymilk powder, water, soymilk to a blender, and process until well-mixed. Transfer the soymilk mixture to a small saucepan, add sugar, vanilla, vinegar, and mi. Cook on medium-low heat, constantly stirring until the mixture is thick and syrupy.

Transfer the mixture to a 9x5-inch loaf pan and freeze uncovered for 1 hour, then return to the blender and blend for 30 seconds until the mixture is creamy. Pour the mixture back in the loaf pan and freeze.

Do this three more times at intervals of 30 minutes, and on the last blend, allow the ice cream to freeze covered for 1 hour.

Serve topped with desired toppings.

## Blueberry Ice Cream

*Prep time: 15 mins*

*Cook time: 15 mins*

*Freeze time: 6 hours*

*Total time: 6 hours 30 mins*

**Ingredients**

14-oz of sweetened condensed milk

¼ cup of granulated sugar

3 cups of heavy cream

Juice and zest of 1 lemon

4 cup of blueberries, plus more for serving

**Directions**

Puree the blueberries in a blender then pour into a medium saucepan. Place the saucepan on medium-high heat, add sugar, lemon juice, lemon zest and bring to a boil. Lower the heat and simmer for 15 minutes until slightly reduced. Pour the mixture into a bowl and chill in the fridge for 1 to 2 hours.

Add the heavy cream in a large bowl, whisk until stiff peaks form, fold in the condensed milk, then the chilled blueberry puree until well mixed.

Pour the mixture in a 9x5-inch loaf pan and freeze for 5 hours.

Serve topped with fresh blueberries.

## Coffee Ice Cream

*Prep time: 15 mins*

*Freeze time: 6 hours*

*Total time: 6 hours 15 mins*

### Ingredients

2 cups of heavy cream

1 teaspoon of vanilla extract

14-ounce can of sweetened condensed milk

1 pinch of kosher salt

¼ cup of hot water

2 tablespoons of instant espresso granules

### Directions

Into a medium-sized bowl, add the hot water and then whip in the espresso granules until dissolved. Beat in the condensed milk, vanilla extract, and salt until well combined, then chill in the fridge.

Meanwhile, whisk the heavy cream until stiff peaks form.

Stir in the chilled milk mixture until well combined, then transfer the mixture to a loaf pan and cover with plastic wrap. Freeze for 6 hours or overnight for best results.

Serve garnished with chocolate chips, cookies, or any other desired toppings.

## Vegan Peanut Butter Ice Cream

*Prep time: 10 mins*

*Freeze time: 2 hours*

*Total time: 2 hours 10 mins*

**Ingredients**

¼ cup of smooth peanut butter

¼ teaspoon of ground cinnamon

1 pinch of kosher salt

1 tablespoon of coconut oil

4 very ripe bananas

¼ teaspoon of grated nutmeg

**Directions**

Cut bananas into ¼-thick rounds and transfer to a Ziplock bag.

Freeze the slices for 2 hours or overnight, making sure you arrange them in a single flat so that they don't clump together.

# Homemade Ice Cream Recipes

Put the frozen bananas pieces in a blender, add the peanut butter, coconut oil, cinnamon, nutmeg, salt, and blend, then allow the mixture to sit in the blender for 3 minutes before pureeing until creamy.

If you want a firmer ice cream consistency, transfer the mixture to an airtight container and freeze for 1 hour.

## Cookie Butter Ice Cream

*Prep time: 5 mins*

*Freeze time: 4 hours*

*Total time: 4 hours 5 mins*

### Ingredients

2 cups of crumbled Biscoff cookies, divided

14-oz can of sweetened condensed milk

¼ cup of Biscoff cookie butter

3 cups of heavy whipping cream

### Directions

Place the cream and the condensed milk in a large bowl and whisk until stiff peaks form.

Gradually fold in the cookie butter until well mixed, top with the cup of crumbled cookies and fold in. Transfer the mixture into a loaf pan and freeze for 4 hours. Serve garnished with the rest of the crumbled cookie.

# Raspberry Ice Cream

*Prep time: 5 mins*

*Total time: 5 mins*

## Ingredients

2 cups of frozen raspberries

1/3 cup of powdered erythritol

1 cup of heavy cream

## Directions

Transfer the cream into a blender and process until stiff peaks form. Add in the frozen raspberries and powdered erythritol, and process until well incorporated. Test for sweetness, and if you want add more powdered erythritol, pulse until well-mixed.

For firmer ice cream, freeze, stirring every 30-60mins to break any ice crystal that forms.

## Snow Ice Cream

*Prep time: 5 mins*

*Freeze time: 1 hour*

*Total time: 1 hour 5 mins*

### Ingredients

4 cups of snow

1/3 cup of sugar

1 teaspoon of pure vanilla extract

1 cup of sweetened condensed milk

Sprinkles for garnishing (optional)

### Directions

Place the condensed milk, sugar, and vanilla extract in a bowl and whisk until smooth.

Transfer the milk mixture into a large bowl with snow and mix well. Place in the freezer for 30-60 minutes. Serve garnished with sprinkles.

# Keto-Coconut Ice Cream

*Prep time: 15 mins*

*Freeze time: 5 hours*

*Total time: 5 hours 15 mins*

## Ingredients

¼ cup of Swerve confectioner's sweetener

1 pinch of kosher salt

30-oz. of coconut milk

1 teaspoon of pure vanilla extract

2 cups of heavy cream

## Directions

Refrigerate the coconut milk for 3 hours or overnight.

To make the whipped coconut, scoop out the coconut cream, leave the liquid in the can, and whisk in a large bowl until very creamy, then put aside.

Pour the heavy cream into a different bowl and whisk until soft peaks form, then whisk in the sweetener and vanilla.

Fold the whipped coconut cream into the whipped cream, then pour the mixture into a loaf pan and freeze for 5 hours.

## Unicorn Ice Cream

*Prep time: 20 mins*

*Freeze time: 5 hours*

*Total time: 5 hours 20 mins*

### Ingredients

11-oz. of sweetened condensed milk

2 drops of pink, purple, green, blue, yellow food coloring

1 teaspoon of pure vanilla extract

3 cups of heavy cream

Sprinkles (optional for topping)

### Directions

Whip the heavy cream until medium peaks form. Pour in the condensed milk and vanilla extract, fold in until well mixed, then pour out the mixture into 5 bowls. Add food coloring to each bowl and mix until combined.

In a 9x5-inch loaf pan, layer all the colored mixture. Swirl a knife in the mixture, lightly mixing the colors, and then smoothen the top.

Top with sprinkles of choice and freeze for 5 hours. Let the ice cream soften for 5 to 10 minutes before serving.

# Maple Bacon Ice Cream

*Prep time: 20 mins*

*Freeze time: 6 hours*

*Total time: 6 hours 20 mins*

## Ingredients

2 tablespoons of Maple syrup

1 teaspoon of vanilla extract

1 pint of heavy cream

½ teaspoon of maple extract

1 cup of brown sugar

½ pound bacon

14-ounce can of sweetened condensed milk

## Directions

Preheat your oven to 400F.

Place the brown sugar on a plate, then coat both sides of the bacon with the sugar.

Spray a cooling rack with non-stick cooking spray, then place the sugar-coated bacon.

Transfer the cooling rack to a baking sheet layered with aluminum foil. Place in the oven and bake until the bacon strips caramelize and are firm, which should take about 15 to 20 minutes. Allow the bacon to cool and transfer onto parchment paper for further cooling.

Whisk the cream until firm peaks form. Add in the condensed milk, vanilla extract, maple extract, and then mix gently until well combined.

Transfer the mixture to a large casserole dish, top with the chopped, candied bacon, and freeze for 6 hours.

Serve drizzled with the maple syrup.

# Colorful Ice Cream

*Prep time: 20 mins*

*Freeze time: 5 hours*

*Total time: 5 hours 20 mins*

## Ingredients

14-oz. of sweetened condensed milk

Green, blue, and purple food coloring

1 teaspoon of pure vanilla extract

3 cups of heavy cream

Sprinkles, for garnishing

## Directions

Whisk the heavy cream until medium peaks form. Add in the condensed milk and vanilla, then fold in until well combined.

Pour the mixture into 5 bowls, and in each bowl, add in different amounts of the food coloring and mix well.

In a 9x5-inch loaf pan, layer the mixture.

Swirl a knife through the mixture to mix the colors, then smoothen the top.

# Homemade Ice Cream Recipes

Top with sprinkles and place the loaf pan in the freezer for 5 hours.

Allow to soften for 5-10 minutes before serving, then scoop and enjoy!

# Conclusion

We have come to the end of the book. Thank you for reading, and congratulations on reading until the end.

If you found the book valuable, can you recommend it to others? One way to do that is to post a review on Amazon.

Please leave a review for this book on Amazon by visiting the page below:

https://amzn.to/2VMR5qr

Thank you, and good luck!

Printed in Great Britain
by Amazon